Conference of the North American Chapter of the Association for Computational Linguistics: Human Language Technologies (NAACL HLT 2015)

Tutorial Abstracts

AA005705

Denver, Colorado, USA
31 May – 5 June 2015

ISBN: 978-1-5108-0446-3

Printed from e-media with permission by:

Curran Associates, Inc.
57 Morehouse Lane
Red Hook, NY 12571

Some format issues inherent in the e-media version may also appear in this print version.

Printed by Curran Associates, Inc. (2015)

For permission requests, please contact the Association for Computational Linguistics at the address below.

Association for Computational Linguistics
209 N. Eighth Street
Stroudsburg, Pennsylvania 18360

Phone: 1-570-476-8006
Fax: 1-570-476-0860

acl@aclweb.org

Additional copies of this publication are available from:

Curran Associates, Inc.
57 Morehouse Lane
Red Hook, NY 12571 USA
Phone: 845-758-0400
Fax: 845-758-2634
Email: curran@proceedings.com
Web: www.proceedings.com

Introduction

This volume contains the abstracts for the tutorials presented at NAACL 2015. This year we held a joint call for tutorials for NAACL, ACL and EMNLP. We received a total of 32 proposals that were reviewed by the six tutorial co-chairs. After careful deliberation six tutorials were accepted to be presented at NAACL.

We are grateful to Rada Mihalcea, NAACL general chair, Peter Ljunglof, NAACL website chair, Saif M. Mohammad, NAACL publicity chair, Matt Post, NAACL publications chair, and Priscilla Rasmussen, local arrangement chair for their help during the whole process. We also want to extend our sincere gratitude to the other tutorial chairs: Eneko Agirre, Kevin Duh, Maggie Li, and Khalil Sima'an. Last, but not least, we thank the tutorial presenters for their effort in developing these great tutorials.

We hope you enjoy the tutorial program!

NAACL 2015 Tutorial co-chairs
Yang Liu
Thamar Solorio

Tutorial Co-chairs:

Yang Liu, The University of Texas at Dallas
Thamar Solorio, University of Houston

Table of Contents

Conference Program

Sunday, May 31

Morning Session

09:00–12:30 *Hands-on Learning to Search for Structured Prediction*
Hal Daumé III, John Langford, Kai-Wei Chang, He He and Sudha Rao

09:00–12:30 *Crowdsourcing for NLP*
Chris Callison-Burch, Lyle Ungar and Ellie Pavlick

09:00–12:30 *The Logic of AMR: Practical, Unified, Graph-Based Sentence Semantics for NLP*
Nathan Schneider, Jeffrey Flanigan and Tim O'Gorman

Afternoon Session

14:00–17:30 *Deep Learning and Continuous Representations for Natural Language Processing*
Wen-tau Yih, Xiaodong He and Jianfeng Gao

14:00–17:30 *Social Media Predictive Analytics*
Svitlana Volkova, Benjamin Van Durme, David Yarowsky and Yoram Bachrach

14:00–17:30 *Getting the Roles Right: Using FrameNet in NLP*
Collin Baker, Nathan Schneider, Miriam R L Petruck and Michael Ellsworth

Hands-on Learning to Search for Structured Prediction

Hal Daumé III[1], John Langford[2], Kai-Wei Chang[3], He He[1], Sudha Rao[1]
[1] University of Maryland, College Park
[2] Microsoft Research, New York
[3] University of Illinois, Urbana-Champaign
me@hal3.name jl@hunch.net kchang10@illinois.edu
hhe@cs.umd.edu raosudha@cs.umd.edu

1 Introduction

Many problems in natural language processing involve building outputs that are structured. The predominant approach to structured prediction is "global models" (such as conditional random fields), which have the advantage of clean underlying semantics at the cost of computational burdens and extreme difficulty in implementation. An alternative strategy is the "learning to search" (L2S) paradigm, in which the structured prediction task is cast as a sequential decision making process.

One can then devise training-time algorithms that learn to make near optimal collective decisions. This paradigm has been gaining increasing traction over the past five years: most notably in dependency parsing (e.g., MaltParser, ClearNLP, etc.), but also much more broadly in less "sequential" tasks like entity/relation classification and even graph prediction problems found in social network analysis and computer vision.

This tutorial has precisely one goal: an attendee should leave the tutorial with hands on experience writing small programs to perform structured prediction for a variety of tasks, like sequence labeling, dependency parsing and, time-permitting, more.

2 Format

This tutorial is unique (to our knowledge) among ACL tutorials in this regard: half of the time spent will be in the style of a "flipped classroom" in which attendees get hands on experience writing structured predictors on their own or in small groups. All course materials (software, exercises, hints, solutions, etc., will be made available at prior to the event so that students can download the required data ahead of time; we will also bring copies on USB in case there is a problem with the internet).

3 Contents

The first half of the tutorial will be mostly "lecture" style, in which we will cover the basics of how learning to search works for structured prediction. The goal is to provide enough background information that students can understand how to write and debug their own predictors, but the emphasis will not be on how to build new machine learning algorithms. This will also include a brief tutorial on the basics of Vowpal Wabbit, to the extent necessary to understand its structured prediction interface. The second half of the tutorial will focus on hands-on exploration of structured prediction using the Vowpal Wabbit python "learning to search" interface; a preliminary python notebook explaining the interface can be viewed at `http://tinyurl.com/pyvwsearch`; an elaborated version of this notebook will serve as the backbone for the "hands on" part of the tutorial, paired with exercises.

Proceedings of the 2015 NAACL-HLT: Tutorial Abstracts, page 1,
Denver, Colorado, May 31 – June 5, 2015. ©2015 Association for Computational Linguistics

Crowdsourcing for NLP

Chris Callison-Burch, Lyle Ungar, and Ellie Pavlick
Computer and Information Science Department
University of Pennsylvania

1 Introduction

Crowdsourced applications to scientific problems is a hot research area, with over 10,000 publications in the past five years. Platforms such as Amazons Mechanical Turk and CrowdFlower provide researchers with easy access to large numbers of workers. The crowds vast supply of inexpensive, intelligent labor allows people to attack problems that were previously impractical and gives potential for detailed scientific inquiry of social, psychological, economic, and linguistic phenomena via massive sample sizes of human annotated data. We introduce crowdsourcing and describe how it is being used in both industry and academia. Crowdsourcing is valuable to computational linguists both (a) as a source of labeled training data for use in machine learning and (b) as a means of collecting computational social science data that link language use to underlying beliefs and behavior. We present case studies for both categories: (a) collecting labeled data for use in natural language processing tasks such as word sense disambiguation and machine translation and (b) collecting experimental data in the context of psychology; e.g. finding how word use varies with age, sex, personality, health, and happiness.

We will also cover tools and techniques for crowdsourcing. Effectively collecting crowdsourced data requires careful attention to the collection process, through selection of appropriately qualified workers, giving clear instructions that are understandable to non-?experts, and performing quality control on the results to eliminate spammers who complete tasks randomly or carelessly in order to collect the small financial reward. We will introduce different crowdsourcing platforms, review privacy and institutional review board issues, and provide rules of thumb for cost and time estimates. Crowdsourced data also has a particular structure that raises issues in statistical analysis; we describe some of the key methods to address these issues.

No prior exposure to the area is required.

2 Presenters' Background

Dr. Chris Callison-Burch is the Aravind K Joshi term assistant professor in the Computer and Information Science Department at the University of Pennsylvania. Before joining Penn, he was a research faculty member at the Center for Language and Speech Processing at Johns Hopkins University for 6 years. He was the Chair of the Executive Board of the North American chapter of the Association for Computational Linguistics (NAACL) from 2011?2013, and he has served on the editorial boards of the journals Transactions of the ACL (TACL) and Computational Linguistics. He is a Sloan Research Fellow, and he has received faculty research awards from Google, Microsoft and Facebook in addition to funding from DARPA and the NSF. Chris teaches a semseter-long course on Crowdsourcing at Penn (http://crowdsourcing?class.org/)

Dr. Lyle Ungar is a Professor of Computer and Information Science at the University of Pennsylvania. He also holds appointments in several other departments in the Engineering, Medicine, and Business Schools. Dr. Ungar received a B.S. from Stanford University and a Ph.D. from M.I.T. He has published over 200 articles and is co-inventor on eight patents.

Proceedings of the 2015 NAACL-HLT: Tutorial Abstracts, pages 2–3,
Denver, Colorado, May 31 – June 5, 2015. ©2015 Association for Computational Linguistics

His current research includes machine learning, data mining, and text mining, and uses social media to better understand the drivers of physical and mental well-being. Lyles research group collects MTurk crowdsourced labels on natural language data such Facebook posts and tweets, which they use for a variety of NLP and psychology studies. Lyle (with collaborators) has given highly successful tutorials on information extraction, sentiment analysis, and spectral methods for NLP at conferences including NAACL, KDD, SIGIR, ICWSM, CIKM, and AAAI. He and his student gave a tutorial on crowdsourcing last year at the Joint Statistical Meetings (JSM)

Ellie Pavlick is a Ph.D. student at the University of Pennsylvania. Ellie received her B.A. in economics from the Johns Hopkins University, where she began working with Dr. Chris Callison-?Burch on using crowdsourcing to create low? cost training data for statistical machine translation by hiring nonprofessional translators and post-editors. Her current research interests include entailment and paraphrase recognition, for which she has looked at using MTurk to provide more difficult linguistic annotations such as discriminating between fine-grained lexical entailment relations and identifying missing lexical triggers in FrameNet. Ellie TAed and helped design the curriculum for the Crowdsourcing and Human Computation course at Penn.

3 Learning Objectives

Participants will learn to:

- identify where crowdsourcing is and is not useful
- use best practices to design MTurk applications for creating training sets and for conducting natural language experiments
- analyze data collected using MTurk and similar sources
- critically read research that uses crowdsourcing

4 Topics

- Taxonomy of crowdsourcing and human computation. Categorization system: motivation, quality control, aggregation, human skill, process flow. Overview of uses of crowdsourcing
- The Mechanical Turk crowdsourcing platform. Terminology and mechanics: Turkers, Requesters, HITs, micropayments. Demographics and motivation of Mechanical Turk workers.
- The human computation process. Design of experiments, selection of software, cost estimation, privacy/IRB considerations.
- Designing HITs. Writing clear instructions, using qualifications, pricing HITs, approving/rejecting work.
- Quality control. Agreement-?based methods, embedded quality control questions, applying the EM algorithm to find the correct label. When to invest extra funds in quality control versus when to collect more singularly labeled data
- Statistical analysis of MTurk results. Accounting for the block structure and non random sampling of the data
- Case Studies in NLP. Word sense disambiguation, machine translation, information extraction, computational social science

The Logic of AMR: Practical, Unified, Graph-Based Sentence Semantics for NLP

Tutorial at NAACL-HLT 2015

May 31, 2015 in Denver, Colorado

Nathan Schneider, Jeffrey Flanigan, and Tim O'Gorman

Abstract

The Abstract Meaning Representation formalism is rapidly emerging as an important practical form of structured sentence semantics which, thanks to the availability of large-scale annotated corpora, has potential as a convergence point for NLP research. This tutorial unmasks the design philosophy, data creation process, and existing algorithms for AMR semantics. It is intended for anyone interested in working with AMR data, including parsing text into AMRs, generating text from AMRs, and applying AMRs to tasks such as machine translation and summarization.

The goals of this tutorial are twofold. First, it will describe the nature and design principles behind the representation, and demonstrate that it can be practical for annotation. In **Part I: The AMR Formalism**, participants will be coached in the basics of annotation so that, when working with AMR data in the future, they will appreciate the benefits and limitations of the process by which it was created. Second, the tutorial will survey the state of the art for computation with AMRs. **Part II: Algorithms and Applications** will focus on the task of parsing English text into AMR graphs, which requires algorithms for alignment, for structured prediction, and for statistical learning. The tutorial will also address graph grammar formalisms that have been recently developed, and future applications such as AMR-based machine translation and summarization.

Participants with laptops are encouraged to bring them to the tutorial.

Instructors

Part I: The AMR Formalism

Nathan Schneider is an annotation schemer and computational modeler for natural language. He has been involved in the design of the AMR formalism since 2012, when he interned with Kevin Knight at ISI. His 2014 dissertation introduced a coarse-grained representation for lexical semantics that facilitates rapid annotation and is practical for broad-coverage statistical NLP. He has also worked on semantic parsing for the FrameNet representation and other forms of syntactic/semantic annotation and processing for social media text. For most of these projects, he led the design of the annotation scheme, guidelines, and workflows, and the training and supervision of annotators.

Proceedings of the 2015 NAACL-HLT: Tutorial Abstracts, pages 4–5,
Denver, Colorado, May 31 – June 5, 2015. ©2015 Association for Computational Linguistics

Tim O'Gorman is a third year Linguistics Ph.D. student at the University of Colorado – Boulder, working with Martha Palmer. He manages CU-Boulder's AMR annotation team, and participated in the Fred Jelinek Memorial Workshop in Prague in 2014, working on mapping the Prague tectogrammatical layer to AMRs. His research areas include implicit arguments, semantic role projection, and linking sentence-level semantics to discourse.

Part II: Algorithms and Applications

Jeffrey Flanigan is a fifth year Ph.D. candidate at Carnegie Mellon University. He and his collaborators at CMU built the first broad-coverage AMR parser. He also participated in the Fred Jelinek Memorial Workshop in Prague in 2014, working on cross-lingual parsing and generation from AMR. His research areas include machine translation, generation, summarization, and semantic parsing.

Deep Learning and Continuous Representations for Natural Language Processing

Scott Wen-tau Yih, Xiaodong He & Jianfeng Gao

Introduction

Deep learning techniques have demonstrated tremendous success in the speech and language processing community in recent years, establishing new state-of-the-art performance in speech recognition, language modeling, and have shown great potential for many other natural language processing tasks. The focus of this tutorial is to provide an extensive overview on recent deep learning approaches to problems in language or text processing, with particular emphasis on important real-world applications including language understanding, semantic representation modeling, question answering and semantic parsing, etc.

In this tutorial, we will first survey the latest deep learning technology, presenting both theoretical and practical perspectives that are most relevant to our topic. We plan to cover common methods of deep neural networks and more advanced methods of recurrent, recursive, stacking and convolutional networks. In addition, we will introduce recently proposed continuous-space representations for both semantic word embedding and knowledge base embedding, which are modeled by either matrix/tensor decomposition or neural networks.

Next, we will review general problems and tasks in text/language processing, and underline the distinct properties that differentiate language processing from other tasks such as speech and image object recognition. More importantly, we highlight the general issues of natural language processing, and elaborate on how new deep learning technologies are proposed and fundamentally address these issues. We then place particular emphasis on several important applications, including (1) machine translation, (2) semantic information retrieval and (3) semantic parsing and question answering. For each task, we will discuss what particular architectures of deep learning models are suitable given the nature of the task, and how learning can be performed efficiently and effectively using end-to-end optimization strategies.

Outline

Part I. Background of neural network learning architectures

- Background: A review of deep learning theory and applications in relevant fields
- Advanced architectures for modeling language structure
- Common problems and concepts in language processing:
    - Why deep learning is needed

Proceedings of the 2015 NAACL-HLT: Tutorial Abstracts, pages 6–8,
Denver, Colorado, May 31 – June 5, 2015. ©2015 Association for Computational Linguistics

    - Concept of embedding
    - Classification/prediction vs. representation/similarity
- Learning techniques: regularization, optimization, GPU, etc.

Part II. Machine translation

- Overview of Machine Translation
- Deep learning translation models for SMT
- Recurrent neural network for language model for SMT
- Sequence to sequence machine translation

Part III. Learning semantic embedding

- Semantic embedding: from words to sentences
- The Deep Structured Semantic Model/Deep Semantic Similarity Model (DSSM)
- DSSM in practice: Information Retrieval, Recommendation, Auto image captioning

Part IV. Natural language understanding

- Continuous Word Representations & Lexical Semantics
- Semantic Parsing & Question Answering
- Knowledge Base Embedding

Part V. Conclusion

Instructor bios

Scott Wen-tau Yih is a Senior Researcher in the Machine Learning Group at Microsoft Research Redmond. His research interests include natural language processing, machine learning and information retrieval. Yih received his Ph.D. in computer science at the University of Illinois at Urbana-Champaign. His work on joint inference using integer linear programming (ILP) [Roth & Yih, 2004] helped the UIUC team win the CoNLL-05 shared task on semantic role labeling, and the approach has been widely adopted in the NLP community. After joining MSR in 2005, he has worked on email spam filtering, keyword extraction and search & ad relevance. His recent work focuses on continuous semantic representations using neural networks and matrix/tensor decomposition methods, with applications in lexical semantics, knowledge base embedding and question answering. Yih received the best paper award from CoNLL-2011 and has served as area chairs (HLT-NAACL-12, ACL-14) and program co-chairs (CEAS-09, CoNLL-14) in recent years.

Xiaodong He is a Researcher of Microsoft Research, Redmond, WA, USA. He is also an Affiliate Professor in Electrical Engineering at the University of Washington, Seattle, WA, USA. His research interests include deep learning, information retrieval, natural language understanding, machine translation, and speech recognition. Dr. He has published a book and more than 70 technical papers in these areas, and has given tutorials at international conferences in these fields. In benchmark evaluations, he and his colleagues have developed entries that obtained No. 1 place in the 2008 NIST

Machine Translation Evaluation (NIST MT) and the 2011 International Workshop on Spoken Language Translation Evaluation (IWSLT), both in Chinese-English translation, respectively. He serves as Associate Editor of IEEE Signal Processing Magazine and IEEE Signal Processing Letters, as Guest Editors of IEEE TASLP for the Special Issue on Continuous-space and related methods in natural language processing, and Area Chair of NAACL2015. He also served as GE for several IEEE Journals, and served in organizing committees and program committees of major speech and language processing conferences in the past. He is a senior member of IEEE and a member of ACL.

Jianfeng Gao is a Principal Researcher of Microsoft Research, Redmond, WA, USA. His research interests include Web search and information retrieval, natural language processing and statistical machine learning. Dr. Gao is the primary contributor of several key modeling technologies that help significantly boost the relevance of the Bing search engine. His research has also been applied to other MS products including Windows, Office and Ads. In benchmark evaluations, he and his colleagues have developed entries that obtained No. 1 place in the 2008 NIST Machine Translation Evaluation in Chinese-English translation. He was Associate Editor of ACM Trans on Asian Language Information Processing, (2007 to 2010), and was Member of the editorial board of Computational Linguistics (2006 – 2008). He also served as area chairs for ACL-IJCNLP2015, SIGIR2015, SIGIR2014, IJCAI2013, ACL2012, EMNLP2010, ACL-IJCNLP 2009, etc. Dr. Gao recently joined Deep Learning Technology Center at MSR-NExT, working on Enterprise Intelligence.

Social Media Predictive Analytics

Svitlana Volkova, Benjamin Van Durme, David Yarowsky, and Yoram Bachrach

The recent explosion of social media services like Twitter, Google+ and Facebook has led to an interest in social media predictive analytics – automatically inferring hidden information from the large amounts of freely available content. It has a number of applications, including: online targeted advertising, personalized marketing, large-scale passive polling and real-time live polling, personalized recommendation systems and search, and real-time healthcare analytics etc.

In this tutorial, we will describe how to build a variety of social media predictive analytics for inferring latent user properties from a Twitter network including demographic traits, personality, interests, emotions and opinions etc. Our methods will address several important aspects of social media such as: dynamic, streaming nature of the data, multi-relationality in social networks, data collection and annotation biases, data and model sharing, generalization of the existing models, data drift, and scalability to other languages.

We will start with an overview of the existing approaches for social media predictive analytics. We will describe the state-of-the-art static (batch) models and features. We will then present models for streaming (online) inference from single and multiple data streams; and formulate a latent attribute prediction task as a sequence-labeling problem. Finally, we present several techniques for dynamic (iterative) learning and prediction using active learning setup with rationale annotation and filtering.

The tutorial will conclude with a practice session focusing on walk-through examples for predicting latent user properties e.g., political preferences, income, education level, life satisfaction and emotions emanating from user communications on Twitter.

Svitlana Volkova is a Ph.D. Candidate in Computer Science at the Center for Language and Speech Processing, Johns Hopkins University. She works on machine learning and natural language processing techniques for social media predictive analytics. She develops batch and streaming (dynamic) models for automatically inferring psycho-demographic profiles from social media data streams, fine-grained emotion detection and sentiment analysis for under-explored languages and dialects in microblogs, effective interactive and iterative rationale annotation via crowdsourcing.

Benjamin Van Durme is the Chief Lead of Text Research at the Human Language Technology Center of Excellence, and an Assistant Research Professor at the Center for Language and Speech Processing. He works on natural language processing (specifically computational semantics), predictive analytics in social media and streaming/randomized algorithms.

David Yarowsky is a Professor at the Center for Language and Speech Processing, Johns Hopkins University. His research interests include natural language processing and spoken language systems, machine translation, information retrieval, very large text databases and machine learning. His research focuses on word sense disambiguation, minimally supervised induction algorithms in NLP, and multilingual natural language processing.

Yoram Bachrach is a researcher in the Online Services and Advertising group at Microsoft Research Cambridge UK. His research area is artificial intelligence (AI), focusing on multi-agent systems and computational game theory. Computational game theory combines the theoretical foundations of economics and game theory with creative solutions from AI and computer science.

Proceedings of the 2015 NAACL-HLT: Tutorial Abstracts, page 9,
Denver, Colorado, May 31 – June 5, 2015.

Getting the Roles Right: Using FrameNet in NLP

Collin F. Baker, Nathan Schneider, Miriam R. L. Petruck, Michael Ellsworth

The FrameNet lexical database (Fillmore & Baker 2010; Ruppenhofer *et al.* 2006) `http://framenet.icsi.berkeley.edu`), covers roughly 13,000 lexical units (word senses) for the core Engish lexicon, associating them with roughly 1,200 fully defined semantic frames; these frames and their roles cover the majority of event types in everyday, non-specialist text, and they are documented with 200,000 manually annotated examples. This tutorial will teach attendees what they need to know to start using the FrameNet lexical database as part of an NLP system. We will cover the basics of Frame Semantics, explain how the database was created, introduce the Python API and the state of the art in automatic frame semantic role labeling systems; and we will discuss FrameNet collaboration with commercial partners. Time permitting, we will present new research on frames and annotation of locative relations, as well as corresponding metaphorical uses, along with information about how frame semantic roles can aid the interpretation of metaphors.

- Introduction
  - FrameNet and its relevance to NLP
  - crucial differences from other resources
    - WordNet
    - PropBank
    - AMR
  - FrameNets in other languages
    - Spanish FN
    - Swedish FN++
    - Japanese FN
    - Multilingual FrameNet
- The Components of Berkeley FrameNet
  - Frames
  - Frame Elements (roles)
  - Frame-to-frame relations
  - Lexicographic annotation
  - Full-text annotation
- Demo of the FrameNet website
- Using the Python API and NLTK integration
- How FrameNet annotation works
  - Vanguarding, subcorporation, and annotation
  - Frame creation
  - Current research on procedural improvements (crowdsourcing, etc.).

Proceedings of the 2015 NAACL-HLT: Tutorial Abstracts, pages 10–12,
Denver, Colorado, May 31 – June 5, 2015.

- Overview of ASRL research (including SEMAFOR)
- Applications of FrameNet/ASRL
  - FN Brasil: World Cup, Olympics
  - DAC collaboration
- Q&A / Discussion

Collin Baker (International Computer Science Institute, collinb@icsi.berkeley.edu), has been Project Manager of the FrameNet Project since 2000. His research interests include FrameNets in other languages (Lönneker-Rodman & Baker 2009), aligning FrameNet to other lexical resources (Fellbaum & Baker 2013; Ferrández *et al.* 2010a), linking to ontologies and reasoning (Scheffczyk *et al.* 2010), and the frame semantics of metaphor.

Nathan Schneider (University of Edinburgh, nschneid@inf.ed.ac.uk, `http://nathan.cl`) has worked on a coarse-grained representation for lexical semantics (2014 dissertation at Carnegie Mellon University) and the design of the Abstract Meaning Representation (AMR; Banarescu et al. 2014). Nathan helped develop the leading open-source frame-semantic parser for English, SEMAFOR (Das et al. 2010, 2014) (`http://demo.ark.cs.cmu.edu/parse`), as well as a Python interface to the FrameNet lexicon (with Chuck Wooters) that is part of the NLTK suite.

Miriam R. L. Petruck (International Computer Science Institute, miriamp@icsi.berkeley.edu) received her PhD in Linguistics from the University of California, Berkeley. A key member of the team developing FrameNet almost since the project's founding, her research interests include semantics, knowledge base development, grammar and lexis, lexical semantics, Frame Semantics and Construction Grammar.

Michael Ellsworth (International Computer Science Institute, infinity@icsi.berkeley.edu) has been involved with FrameNet for well over a decade. His chief focus is on semantic relations in FrameNet (Ruppenhofer *et al.* 2006), how they can be used for paraphrase (Ellsworth & Janin 2007), and mapping to other resources (Scheffczyk & Ellsworth 2006; Ferrández *et al.* 2010b). Increasingly, he has examined the connection of FrameNet to syntax and the Constructicon (Torrent & Ellsworth 2013; Ziem & Ellsworth to appear), including in his pending dissertation on the constructions and frame semantics of emotion.

References

Ellsworth, Michael, & Adam Janin. 2007. Mutaphrase: Paraphrasing with framenet. In *Proceedings of the Workshop on Textual Entailment and Paraphrasing*, Prague. Association for Computational Linguistics.

Fellbaum, Christiane, & Collin Baker. 2013. Comparing and harmonizing different verb classifications in light of a semantic annotation task. *Linguistics* 51.707–728.

Ferrández, Óscar, Michael Ellsworth, Rafael Muñoz, & Collin F. Baker. 2010a. Aligning FrameNet and WordNet based on semantic neighborhoods. In *Proceedings of the Seventh conference on International Language Resources and Evaluation (LREC'10)*, ed. by Nicoletta Calzolari (Conference Chair), Khalid Choukri, Bente Maegaard, Joseph Mariani, Jan Odjik, Stelios Piperidis, Mike Rosner, & Daniel Tapias, 310–314, Valletta, Malta. European Language Resources Association (ELRA).

Ferrández, Oscar, Michael Ellsworth, Rafael Muñoz, & Collin F. Baker. 2010b. A graph-based measure of FrameNet-WordNet alignment. In *Proceedings of ICGL 2010, Second International Conference on Global Interoperability for Language Resources*, Hong Kong.

Fillmore, Charles J., & Collin F. Baker. 2010. A frames approach to semantic analysis. In *Oxford Handbook of Linguistic Analysis*, ed. by Bernd Heine & Heiko Narrog, 313–341. OUP.

Lönneker-Rodman, Birte, & Collin F. Baker. 2009. The FrameNet model and its applications. *Natural Language Engineering* 15.415–453.

Ruppenhofer, Josef, Michael Ellsworth, Miriam R. L. Petruck, Christopher R. Johnson, & Jan Scheffczyk. 2006. *FrameNet II: Extended Theory and Practice*. Berkeley, California: International Computer Science Institute. Distributed with the FrameNet data.

Scheffczyk, Jan, Collin F. Baker, & Srini Narayanan. 2010. Reasoning over natural language text by means of FrameNet and ontologies. In *Ontology and the Lexicon: A Natural Language Processing Perspective*, ed. by Chu-Ren Huang, Nicoletta Calzolari, Aldo Gangemi, Alessandro Lenci, Alessandro Oltramari, & Laurent Prévot, Studies in Natural Language Processing, chapter 4, 53–71. Cambridge, UK: Cambridge University Press. Expanded version of paper at OntoLex, 2006. (ISBN-13: 9780521886598).

——, & Michael Ellsworth. 2006. Improving the quality of framenet. In *Proceedings of the Workshop on Quality assurance and quality measurement for language and speech resources*, ed. by Steven Krauwer & Uwe Quasthoff, 8–13, Genoa, Italy. LREC.

Torrent, Tiago, & Michael Ellsworth. 2013. Behind the labels: Criteria for defining analytical categories in FrameNet Brasil. *Veredas* 17.44–65.

Ziem, Alexander, & Michael Ellsworth. to appear. Exklamativsätze im framenet-konstruktikon am beispiel des englischen. In *Satztypen und Constructionen im Deutschen*, ed. by Rita Finkbeiner & Jörg Meibauer.

Author Index